Social Anxiety

7 Easy Ways to Overcome Your Inferiority Complex TODAY

By

Stuart Killan

© **Copyright 2018 Stuart Killan - All rights reserved.**

The content contained within this book may not be reproduced, duplicated or transmitted without direct written permission from the author or the publisher.

Under no circumstances will any blame or legal responsibility be held against the publisher, or author, for any damages, reparation, or monetary loss due to the information contained within this book. Either directly or indirectly.

Legal Notice:

This book is copyright protected. This book is only for personal use. You cannot amend, distribute, sell, use, quote or paraphrase any part, or the content within this book, without the consent of the author or publisher.

Disclaimer Notice:

Please note the information contained within this document is for educational and entertainment purposes only. All effort has been executed to present accurate, up to date, and reliable, complete information. No warranties of any kind are declared or implied. Readers acknowledge that the author is not engaging in the rendering of legal, financial, medical or professional advice. The content within this book has been derived from various sources. Please consult a licensed professional before attempting any techniques outlined in this book.

By reading this document, the reader agrees that under no circumstances is the author responsible for any losses, direct or indirect, which are incurred as a result of the use of information contained within this document, including, but not limited to, — errors, omissions, or inaccuracies.

Table Of Contents

Your Free Gift

Introduction

Chapter One: The Inferiority Complex

   Difference between Feeling Inferior and the Inferiority Complex

   Types of Inferiority

Chapter Two: Signs of an Inferiority Complex

   Being Sensitive

   Constantly Comparing Your Qualities

   Submissive Behavior

   Perfectionism

   Inaction and Procrastination

   Triggers of Guilt, Shame or Jealousy through Social Media

   You Judge Others

   Try to Hide Flaws without Success

Chapter Three: How to Stop Being Inferior

Check Your Life Circle

Always Replace the Negativity

Your Complex can be Your Desire to be Like Someone Else

Stop Believing that a Flaw is the Root Cause to Your Problems

Identify What Makes You Feel Good about Yourself

Ask Someone You Know to List Your Best Qualities

Focus on Your Successes

Conclusion

Your Free Gift

As a way of saying thank you for downloading. I'm offering a free bonus report called *7 Habits of Highly Confident People* that's exclusive to the readers of this book.

Get instant access at http://freeconfidencebook.com

Inside the book you'll discover

- Secrets of The Joker, and why he should be admired
- The one thing confident people *always* do first when confronted with a tough situation – learning this alone can 10X your self esteem
- How to use vision boards to achieve your goals
- Identifying your "hidden talents" – even if you don't think you have any

- The one trait you must MURDER if you are to become successful
- How to never doubt your own abilities again
- Michael Jordan's #1 success secret
- The 4 most dangerous words in your vocabulary (if you're saying these regularly you are killing your own confidence)
- How to succeed as an introvert in an extrovert's world

Download for free at http://freeconfidencebook.com

Introduction

Thank you for purchasing this book, 'Social Anxiety: 7 Easy Ways to Overcome Your Inferiority Complex TODAY.'

Inferiority complex is why most people find it afraid to take chances since they feel unworthy. People with an inferiority complex are always negative, and this is a characteristic that develops since their childhood. They hide their pain and fear in their heart and mind. They find a way to develop some defense mechanisms to hide these insecurities, or build a wall around them that prevents others from seeing their weakness.

This book provides insights on what an inferiority complex is, and how it develops. You can also identify the signs of the development of an inferiority complex. These signs will help you check your responses to the situations that bring painful memories to your mind. There are some strategies you can use that will help you replace those memories with positive ones. You can also identify ways that will help you avoid being in such situations.

Over the course of this book, you will gather information on what the inferiority complex is, and how people develop that complex. There are some signs that people with an inferiority complex show. If you display any of the signs mentioned in this book, use the methods given in the last chapter to come out of feeling inferior to the people around you.

If you have some issues with self-esteem and often feel inferior, read on and you can have a more confident life!

Thank you for purchasing this book. I hope you enjoy it.

Chapter One: The Inferiority Complex

People often feel inferior at some point in their life. You may have felt inferior to a colleague, sibling or even a friend. It may have been a minor event for some people, but, for others, it can be the start of a major inferiority complex. This is a condition that begins during their childhood and manifests into every aspect of your life if you do not recognize the symptoms early in life. People who suffer from an inferiority complex are very sensitive and belittle themselves.

People with these limitations should identify, accept and overcome their limitations when they reach a certain age in life, but some constantly remember these limitations either due to peer pressure or because of an authoritative parent or adult. These limitations include emotional responses, cultural differences, physical appearances and some disabilities. These people exhibit some inferiority complex symptoms because of these reminders. To overcome the feelings of inferiority, they develop some defense mechanisms. They employ these mechanisms when people talk about their insecurities.

Difference between Feeling Inferior and the Inferiority Complex

You were inferior when you were a baby. You may scoff at this, but think about it. When you are a baby, you cannot stay alive on your own. You are fully dependent on an adult for your survival. As you grow up, adults who are stronger and more capable than you are surrounding you.

Alfred Adler, a famous psychologist, mentioned that it is a healthy motivation to feel inferior. When you see someone do better than you or receive constructive criticism, you will work hard to eliminate any weakness. When you do this, you motivate yourself to do better and feel more powerful; thereby removing any feeling of inferiority. When you feel inferior, you learn from the people around you; therefore, you work towards developing yourself and will eventually become a confident adult.

However, for some people, this feeling of inferiority overpowers them and it stops being useful or helpful. This is what psychologists call the inferiority complex. This complex paralyzes you and prevents you from doing things that you will be good at; thereby resulting in social anxiety or shyness. You may also begin to feel worthless and the fear of failure will prevent you from trying to do something in your life.

That is the difference between the inferiority complex and feeling inferior. When you feel inferior, you can improve the way you work and your life; however, if you have an inferiority complex, it means you feel incomplete and unworthy to work on tasks that you are good at performing. You also find it difficult to visualize that you will achieve something in the future.

Types of Inferiority

People follow a common pattern if they have an inferiority complex. Based on these patterns, people with an inferiority complex fall into two categories:

- People who know that they are good looking, successful and smart, and yet feel inferior. This feeling is mysterious because they believe they are not good enough, but do not know why they feel that way. If this is how you feel, the people around you will tell you, "You are so smart/successful/ beautiful/etc. I really do not know why you feel this way." The unfortunate thing is that you do not understand why you feel that way either; you just feel that way.

- People who know they are dumb, ugly, failures, boring, etc. and their flaws make it difficult for them to receive the friendship, affection and support from others. If you feel this way, you will learn to believe that you can solve any problem that you have if you were smart, good looking and successful, or whatever other reason you tell yourself. Here is a quick test – how would you complete the following sentence: "I will be confident, attractive and happy, if only I was _____."

Which category do you think you fall into? People in the first category feel that it is unrealistic that they are good at what they do. The people in the second category feel the way they do because they only focus on their flaws. Regardless of the category you fall in, you may have been stuck with this feeling for most of your life.

Chapter Two: Signs of an Inferiority Complex

Being Sensitive

If you are inferior, comments about your work or you will send you into a path of depression and self-hate for days or weeks. You feel miserable when someone rejects you or excludes you from any conversation. You want to stop caring about what someone says, but it is not that simple for you.

You may have read many articles on how to handle such comments. Most of these articles advise you to stop worrying about what someone says by giving you a rational argument. You may have come across multiple articles that tell you that another person's opinion about you does not matter. This advice does not help since it is difficult for people to reason their way out of feeling something that they did not force themselves into feeling in the first place.

The solution to stop being too sensitive to what people say about you is not to care less about their opinion. Instead, it is about caring more about what you think of yourself. People who do not care about what someone has to say about them only trust their values.

When your sense of judgment becomes stronger, you stop worrying about what someone has to say about you. This is important to learn, and it takes time for people to find their beliefs and stick to them. You may have heard people telling you that men or women who know who they are are very attractive. You may not have known what that meant. All they meant was that a person is attractive if he or she is firmly rooted to his or her core beliefs. This means that the person is not a pushover and only performs those actions and tasks that adhere to his beliefs.

Constantly Comparing Your Qualities

When you constantly compare your qualities with another person, you feel inferior or superior to them. This is an obvious fact. Let us take a closer look at the problem. Why do you believe that everybody is always more successful and better when compared to you? This is because you focus only on their best quality and compare yourself using that quality as the criterion.

You should remember that a person who is great at one thing is certainly going to be better than you at performing that task since he or she is good at it. For instance, if someone spends at least an hour at the gym, he or she is going to have a better body than you. If a classmate of yours tops every semester, it is because he or she works hard and prepares for the exam well.

You look at these people and tell yourself that you are worse than they are, and then feel inferior. Yes, it is true that you are not going to be as good as they are. This is because you are measuring your success and qualities against constantly changing criteria. You should remember that you could only be successful if you work hard in that area. This means that the people you are comparing yourself with probably neglect other areas of life.

You should always settle for being the best version of yourself. This will relieve you of your need to always meet another's standards. You are not superior or inferior, but are just you.

Submissive Behavior

There is a concept called social rank theory in psychology. This concept says that a person often acts the way he or she does and feels a specific way based on how they perceive their social rank or status to be. When you feel inferior to somebody, or think you have a low status when compared to others, you will begin to act submissive.

Most of the traits of a person who is shy are like that of someone who is submissive. Think of how people who are shy often act:

- Can never make eye contact
- Always talk softly
- Are afraid to assert their opinions

If a chimpanzee was to act this way, a scientist would label it as being submissive. This is where low confidence stems. Submissive people have an unconscious belief that stems from their core. They believe that people are superior, better and deserve more respect when compared to them. If you can overcome this feeling of insecurity, you will find it easier to be outgoing. A study conducted by Paul Gilbert explored the association between social anxiety, shame and depression using the social rank theory as the basis. The theory argues that a person's perception of social status and rank affects his or her mood and emotions. The results of this study confirmed that social anxiety, shame and depression are closely related to submissive behavior and the feeling of inferiority.

Perfectionism

Perfectionism and inferiority go together since they are rooted in comparison. If you are a perfectionist, you will never be happy with what you do. Let us consider the following scenario:

There was a boy named Joe who wanted to be an artist. He was a perfectionist and he believed that this quality would help him become the best artist there ever was; however, perfection doesn't make you best. Joe liked to visit online galleries and forums where he observed the work of some of the best artists across the globe. He believed that his work was terrible when compared to the work that they did. He felt that none of the work that he did would ever match up to the work that they did. He did not find the need to work any longer since his work will never be perfect. According to him, none of the famous artists in those galleries would appreciate his work. His comparison became unhealthy and he began to feel inferior to his competitors. He stopped painting because of this feeling of inferiority. For years he did not pick up a brush because he knew his work would never measure up to his competitors' work.

Perfectionism often worsens the quality of work. It is true that people are born with some qualities and abilities; however, people do not excel in their field only because of hard work. This is a myth that the society is slowly busting. Malcolm Gladwell said that it takes a person at least 10,000 hours to reach a certain level of greatness or genius in an industry. The artists that Joe had admired were in their late 50s, so they spent years making mediocre art before they made their masterpieces.

Inaction and Procrastination

When you want to be perfect at what you do, you may want to stop working on the task, and therefore procrastinate. When you compare yourself with others, and have high standards for yourself, you are not going to work better. You are shooting yourself in the foot.

Since you are afraid of failure, you stop trying. You forget that it takes at least a few failures before you become successful, and you choose to try nothing and accomplish nothing. You apply this fear to every aspect of your life. For instance, since you are socially awkward, you will refrain from meeting new people; however, only when you meet new people and make conversations can you overcome your shyness. If you avoid beating yourself up, you can develop some social skills soon. You should remember that it is okay to be bad at something, since that is the first step at being good at it.

Triggers of Guilt, Shame or Jealousy through Social Media

When you see how people are living their lives on Instagram and Facebook, you begin to feel inferior and start doubting yourself. For instance:

- You see that your friends at college are out partying and are socializing, while you stay at home.

- You see that all your friends are starting their families. This makes you question if you are making the right decisions.

- Your friends have many likes on their posts, but that makes you feel worthless or insignificant since you do not receive those many likes for your posts.

It is important to remember that people always use social media to present the perfect parts of their lives; therefore, you are always making a comparison of your life against one version of their life. You forget that these people have edited all the sad and boring parts of their life. Studies conducted on social media conclude that social media make people feel worse about themselves. This problem multiplies when you have an inferiority complex. A recent study concluded that using social media either during the day or night reduced the quality of sleep and led to increased anxiety, low self-esteem and depression.

Do not even get me started on magazines or news, since they only show images of the most attractive, wealthy and successful people.

You Judge Others

Let us look at some interesting patterns that you may have noticed. If you know men who have always been unsuccessful with women, they will begin to hate them. If a woman or man is thirty years old and still a virgin, she or he will be upset when they see a happy couple or a group of attractive men or women walk past them. This is because these groups of people remind them of what they feel inferior about – their looks, insecurities and fear of failure around the opposite sex.

When women look at newspapers or magazine covers, and find a skinny supermodel on the cover, she will worry about the unrealistic standards that the society has. She is not trying to understand what makes her mad. The image of the supermodel triggers the feelings of unworthiness and unattractiveness inside her. She may feel that she is not as valuable as the supermodel and not as attractive as she is; therefore, she believes that everybody judges her in the same way. Women believe that their value is solely dependent on their appearance.

Unlike women, men do not always compare their appearances, and nobody knows why. Numerous activists have started to petition against the images in magazines and newspapers. Have you observed the pattern yet? Let us look at one last example.

When people make fun of a millionaire wearing an expensive suit or driving an expensive car, they are trying to cover their feeling of inadequacy since they own a Toyota. However, if they win a lottery, they will certainly buy themselves an expensive car or suit; therefore, the lesson is that inferiority makes you judge another person. When you judge someone, you often try to make yourself feel better. This method backfires since you become spiteful. Start identifying the moments when you condemn other people and feel hateful. This will help you identify what makes you feel worse about yourself. Remember that what you perceive or feel about people around you is a reflection of the emotions and feelings within you. If you do not judge people often, you will not constantly feel judged.

Try to Hide Flaws without Success

People who are often insecure or feel ugly do not try to improve their appearance. They will certainly hide what they are ashamed of.

- They either wear baggy clothing to avoid looking at their body shape.

- Always strike the same pose in a photograph.

- If they have crooked teeth, they may try to avoid smiling at all. If they wear braces, they may either cover their mouth or stop smiling.

- If they feel ugly, women may wear a lot of makeup, but, then again, it differs from one woman to another.

The people in the examples above always worry about how people see them. They also want to control how society perceives them. You only feel stressed out and self-conscious from the constant need to stay alert.

Chapter Three: How to Stop Being Inferior

If you have an inferiority complex, you can use the strategies in this chapter that will help you get on the right track. You must be serious and ensure that you work on changing your life; therefore, you should start changing your behavior. Once you reach this chapter, you should implement the strategies mentioned in the book immediately.

Check Your Life Circle

The first thing you should do is to establish the parts of your life that are working, and those that are not. If you are doing great in your career, but do not have any confidence in your relationship, you should identify a way to improve that area of your life. Ensure that you learn to communicate better or listen better. It is always up to you to decide what part of your life you want to improve. When you change some parts of your life for the better, you will become a changed person.

Always Replace the Negativity

You may be uneducated, clumsy or overweight. That does not suggest that you are unintelligent, or that you cannot be kind to yourself. You must make a list of all the reasons why you put yourself down, and try to find a positive way to say it. Instead of calling yourself clumsy, you should tell yourself, "I have to learn to be more graceful."

You should also make sure that you identify the characteristics and traits that make you feel inferior. Identify the people around you that make you feel inferior. Is it your co-worker, a successful person, or your partner? How do these people make you feel bad about yourself? Is there a new skill you can develop that will help you feel better about yourself?

Your Complex can be Your Desire to be Like Someone Else

It is a great idea to look up to someone, or treat someone as your role model. You may want to learn from them, but you should avoid acting like them because you will lose your individuality. You cannot expect to impersonate someone and yet be who you are. Instead, you should identify the characteristics of the person you admire and try to emulate those characteristics while keeping your individuality. You should not compare yourself with them. Remember that you are you.

Stop Believing that a Flaw is the Root Cause to Your Problems

It is important to stop believing that every

problem in your life is based on one of your flaws. This is an issue that many people face, and it is something they do not want to acknowledge. You must remember that your problems cannot be solved if you get married or lose weight. You must identify the root cause of the problem before you try to solve it.

Identify What Makes You Feel Good about Yourself

Do you feel inferior because you are short when compared to all your friends? You must know that this is not something you can do much about. Try to see what it is about you being short makes you feel inferior to others, and then analyze whether you can do something about this 'flaw.' Try to visualize what it would be like if you can be taller. Does that make you a happier person? Is it something you can relate to? Do you feel like yourself? Do you think you can become taller now?

You should use this technique to visualize your version of the solution. This will help you redefine your problem, and allow you to feel comfortable in your own skin. All you need to do is stay patient.

Ask Someone You Know to List Your Best Qualities

It is easier to ask someone you trust to list your favorite qualities. You know what they are, but you do not trust yourself. It feels great when someone lists your qualities. You will be more confident. There are times when you do not know who you are, but if a friend tells you what the best part about you is, you will feel better about yourself. If you want them to elaborate, ask them to do so. You may want to know why they think that you have a specific quality. Ask them to give you examples.

Focus on Your Successes

Regardless of what your age is, you should focus on your successes, small or big. Every great leader practices this regularly, and you should too. When you go to the gym, stay in touch with an old friend, complete all your tasks for the day or pack a healthy meal, congratulate yourself because they are worthy accomplishments. All of us have failures, but these failures are what help us become successful in the future. The truth is that you are doing better than you think.

People go through their day with the impression that every person around them knows what their flaws are. It is because of this that they feel inferior to the people around them; however, not everybody knows how clumsy you are, because they have their stuff to deal with. They may not have had the time in the world to consider your flaws. The truth is that most people around you are not thinking about you. If you think this is untrue, pay attention to the conversation you have when you are at a family gathering. Most people complain about how terrible their life is. They do not talk about your flaws; therefore, you are free.

Conclusion

Everybody feels inferior at some point in their life. There are many people who will do better than you, but you are doing much better than someone else. You should never let your inferiority complex get the better of you. Ensure that you push yourself to do better, and use that inferiority as a tool to drive you to do better. You must identify ways to develop confidence and use that confidence to be successful.

If you want to conquer your inferiority complex, you should focus on your self-talk, strengths and remember that nobody is watching you. The bottom line is that you can let go of your inferiority and be the best version of yourself without worrying too much about your life.

Thank you for purchasing this book. I hope you become confident and take over the world. I wish you good luck on your journey.

www.ingramcontent.com/pod-product-compliance
Lightning Source LLC
Chambersburg PA
CBHW071507080526
44587CB00016B/2720